RAINBOW
DREAMS
14

EGYPTIAN
SPIRALS
BRACELET
18

RAINBOW
BRACELET
27

Produced by GMC Publications Ltd.
86 High Street, Lewes, East Sussex, BN7 1XN, United Kingdom
www.thegmcgroup.com, +44 (0) 1273 477374

All images supplied by GMC Designs.

We have made every effort to ensure that these instructions are accurate and complete. We cannot, however, be responsible for human error, typographical mistakes, or variations in individual work.

SPIKED CRYSTAL

By Jessica Rose

The garnet and mauve colors used in this project combined with a rich gold add a sophisticated feel to this wrapped statement necklace.

MATERIALS

- 59" length 20 gauge (0.8mm) gold-plated wire
- 26 gauge (0.4mm) garnet red-coated craft wire
- 16 x gold-colored spike charms with looped top
- 5 x 10mm–12mm gold-plated jumprings
- 7 x 6mm–7mm gold-plated jumprings
- Gold-plated clasp
- 40 x 8mm garnet-colored Swarovski xilions
- 2 x 4mm purple velvet Swarovski xilions
- 26 x 6mm purple velvet Swarovski xilions
- 12 x 6mm amethyst Swarovski xilions
- 44 x 4mm gold-plated round beads
- Medium gold-plated round beads (with large center hole)
- Basic jewelry tools
- Beading mat

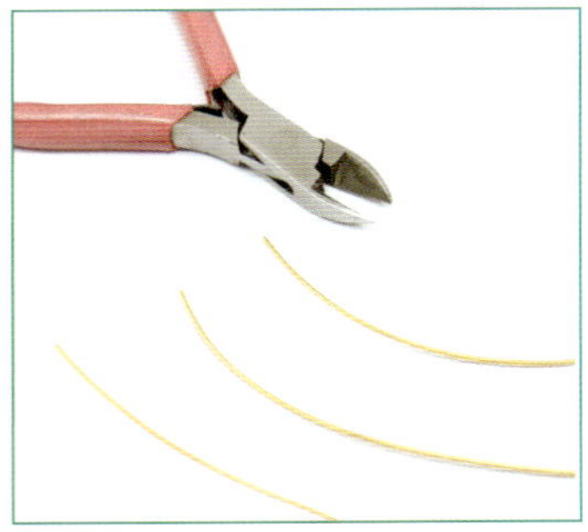

STEP 1

Cut three lengths of 20 gauge gold-plated wire, each approx. 16" in length. Slightly curve the wires with your hands so that each one forms a large, circular shape. These will form the basis of your necklace where you will be wrapping your crystals in the following steps.

STEP 6

Complete a similar process with the other two wires. One of which consists of 31 alternating 6mm purple velvet and 8mm garnet crystals. The other is the small gold-plated round beads with a mix of 6mm purple velvet crystals and 6mm amethyst colored crystals. Wrap each one on individually using the same red-colored wire until you have the complete front of your design as shown.

STEP 2

Take a 39" length of 26 gauge red-colored wire and wrap it around one of the gold wires about a third of the way from one wire end. After nine or ten wraps, thread on an 8mm garnet-colored Swarovski crystal to one side of the wire, holding it in place with your hands as you wrap. Then wrap the red wire back round the gold wire two or three times.

STEP 3

Continue adding crystals down the gold wire towards the center. Each time you add a crystal, wrap the red wire back around the gold two or three times before adding the next one and be sure that all your crystals face the same direction. After five garnet crystals add a gold spike in exactly the same way.

STEP 4

Continue down the gold wire, adding seven spikes with a crystal in between each one. You will then have reached the center of the necklace. Add a symmetrical pattern on the other side, starting with a single garnet crystal in the opposite direction.

STEP 5

You should now have a complete gold wire with crystals and spikes on. To finish the red wire, wrap it nine or ten times around the gold piece at the other side to match the first wrap you made in Step 2. Don't worry about the end of the gold wires for now, they will be completed later on.

PHOTOGRAPHS: LAUREL GUILFOYLE, JESSICA ROSE

STEP 7

Add a cluster of crystals to the middle of the spiked wrapped layer. Use a simple looping technique with round nose pliers starting with one 6mm purple velvet crystal at the top followed by two 6mm amethyst crystals and one 8mm garnet crystal and then two 4mm purple velvet crystals, separated by a spike to finish.

STEP 8

Attach your gold wires together: thread four 4mm round gold beads to the end of each gold wire for spacing and decoration. Then wrap the three gold wires together at either end of the piece using a length of the red-colored wire. Make sure that you line up the three layers of the necklace in a shape and position that you like before wrapping them in place.

STEP 9

To finish, cut the ends of the gold wires down to a length that suits you for the piece (allowing room for a clasp) and loop the ends using your round nose pliers. Attach a large gold-plated jumpring on each side of the piece and the clasp. You could also add a length of jumprings and a final spike to give the piece an adjustable length, which is always a nice finishing touch.

Extra Project Make matching earrings

To make a pair of matching earrings simply recreate the cluster from the center of the necklace and attach a gold-plated earwire on the top. It couldn't be simpler.

FALLING LEAVES

By Kristin Smith

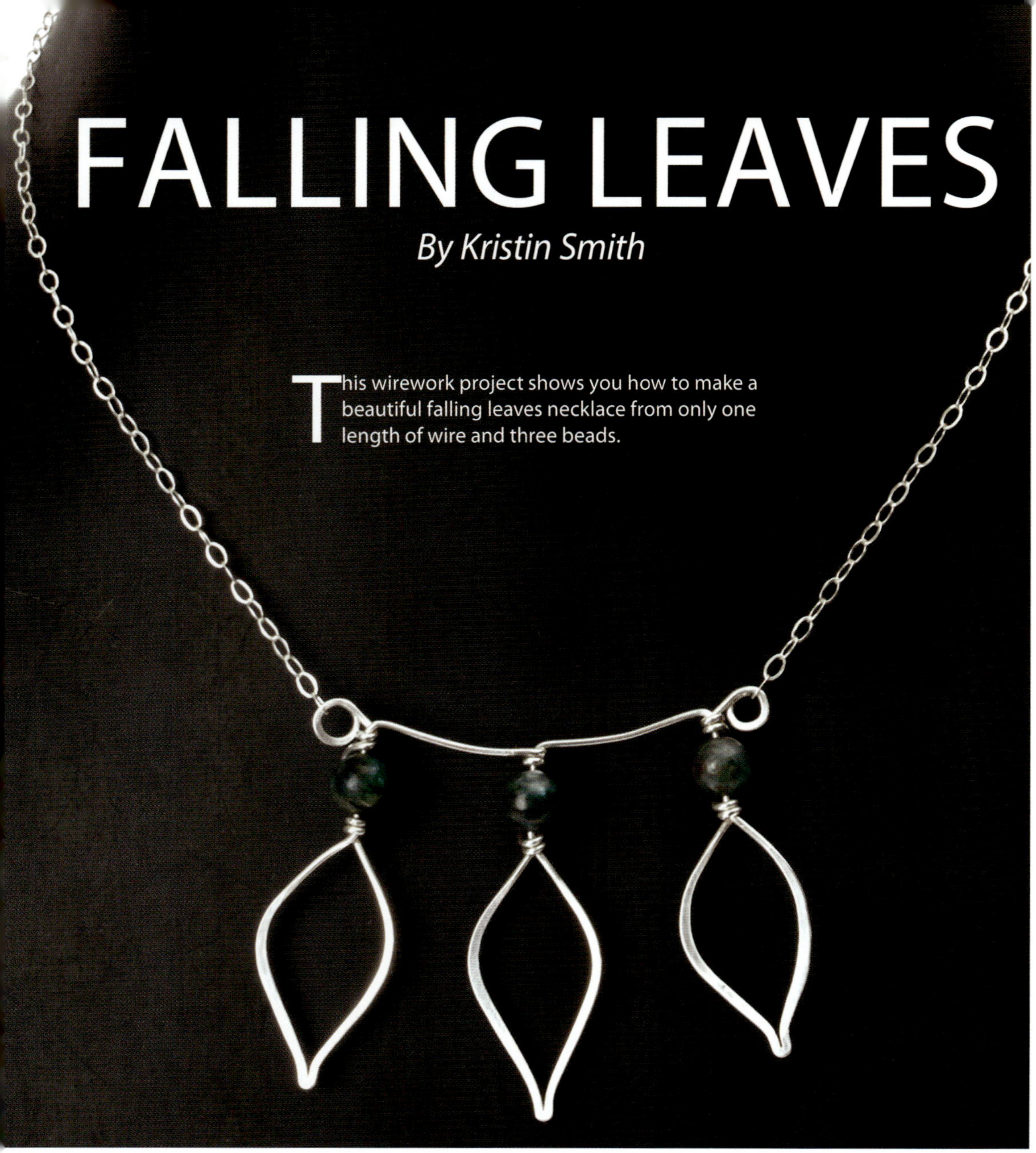

This wirework project shows you how to make a beautiful falling leaves necklace from only one length of wire and three beads.

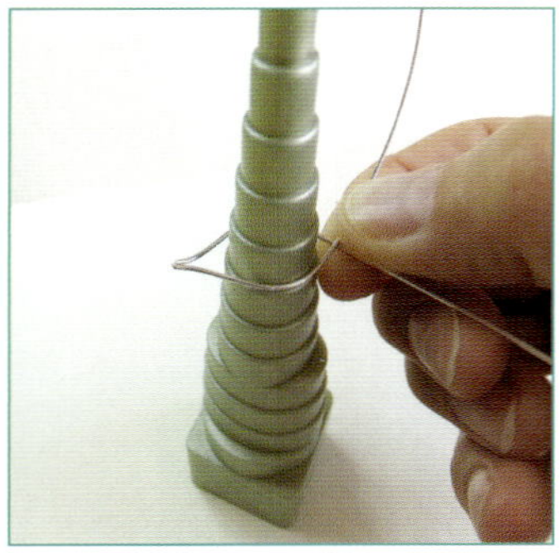

STEP 1

Cut off a 16" length of 20 gauge soft wire. Straighten any kinks by running it through a pair of nylon-headed pliers and clean the wire with a polishing cloth. Bend the wire length in half and pinch the bend with a pair of pliers to make a point. Open up the wire piece to make a large 'V' shape and place it around a dowel approximately 5/8" diameter, letting the wires cross over to make a leaf shape approximately 1 1/4" long.

STEP 6

Pinch the point of the leaf between your chain nose pliers. Use your dowel to help create the shape of the leaf (as in Step 1) and complete the leaf by wrapping the wire twice below the bead, diagonally across the back of the bead and then wrap twice above the bead (as in Steps 3 and 4). Make sure your wraps come from the back to the front of the wire piece to be consistent with the formation of the central leaf.

MATERIALS

- 20 gauge (0.8mm) soft round wire
- 6mm round beads
- Trace chain necklace (medium size links)
- Round dowel (about 5/8" diameter)
- Stainless steel block
- Smooth headed hammer
- Emery papers (rough to smooth)
- Polishing cloth
- Basic jewelry tools

Designer tips

- Soft or dead soft wire is best for this design as the wire needs to be easy to manipulate with your fingers. Plated wire is not recommended due to the hammering and sanding elements of this design.
- To avoid making tool marks in the wire, try not to grip the wire too tightly with your pliers and use your fingers to shape or wrap the wire wherever possible.
- Aim for consistency and neatness of your wire wraps in this project. The wraps at the top of each leaf and above each bead should begin the same way, with the wire coming round the back to the front.
- To avoid hammer marks, make sure your hammer has a very smooth head with slightly curved edges. Always try to hammer straight down and not at an angle.
- For this necklace I have used a 16" trace chain necklace and removed about 2" from the center to allow for the length of the wire piece.

STEP 2

Draw a straight line on a piece of paper. Lay your leaf shape on the paper so that the drawn line runs down the center. This line will guide you where to place the tips of your chain nose pliers. Grip the top wire (which will now be called 'Wire A') with your pliers at the point where it crosses over the bottom wire (now called 'Wire B') and bend the rest of Wire A straight up so it runs parallel to the line on the paper.

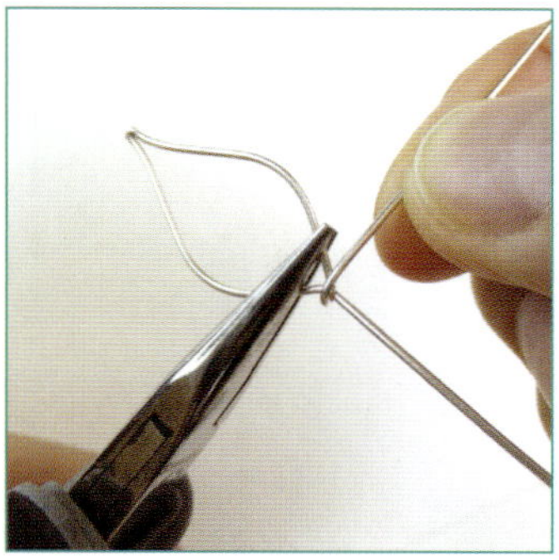

STEP 3

Turn the leaf over so that Wire B lies on top of Wire A. Grip both the wires near the top of the leaf between your chain nose pliers. Now grip Wire B with your fingers and bend it 90 degrees across Wire A. Wrap it twice around Wire A at the top of the leaf.

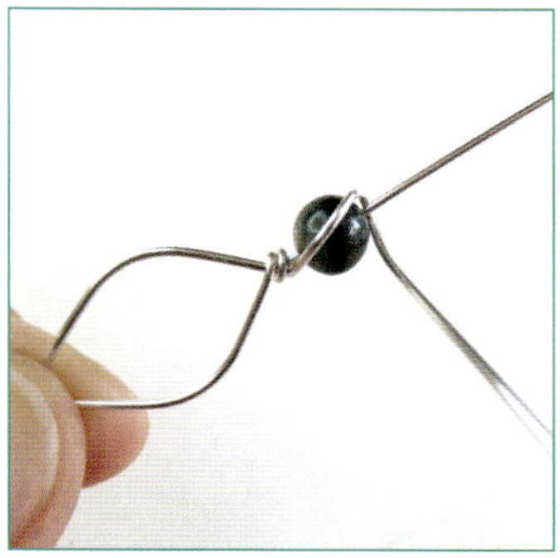

STEP 4

Slide a bead down Wire A. Bring Wire B diagonally across the back of the bead and wrap it twice around Wire A above the bead to secure the bead in place. Now you are ready to make the two leaves that sit either side of the central leaf you have just made. Hold Wire A and Wire B and pull them away from each other so that they make a continuous line across the top of the leaf.

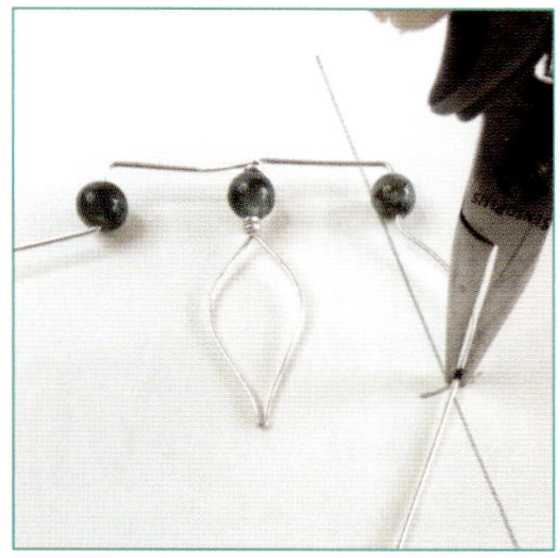

STEP 5

Measure $^{5}/_{8}$" along each wire from the top of the central leaf and make a 90º bend down with your pliers. Slide a bead up each wire and stop them sliding off by making a slight bend in each wire. It is important that you leave about $^{1}/_{8}$" of wire below each bead before you bend it, to leave space for the wrapping you will be making below and above each bead. Also, make sure you bend each wire away from the central leaf. Start forming a second leaf by making a slight curve in the remaining wire and use the line drawn on the paper to guide where to bend the wire to make the point of the leaf.

PHOTOGRAPHS: LAUREL GUILFOYLE, KRISTIN SMITH

STEP 7

After the two wraps above the bead, pull the rest of the wire to the side. Repeat Steps 5 and 6 to create the third leaf. Turn the whole wire piece over and you will notice that one of the beads has the wire lying diagonally across it in the opposite way to the other two beads. Don't worry – this is correct because the wrapping for that leaf was done in a different direction to ensure the wire finishes in the right place.

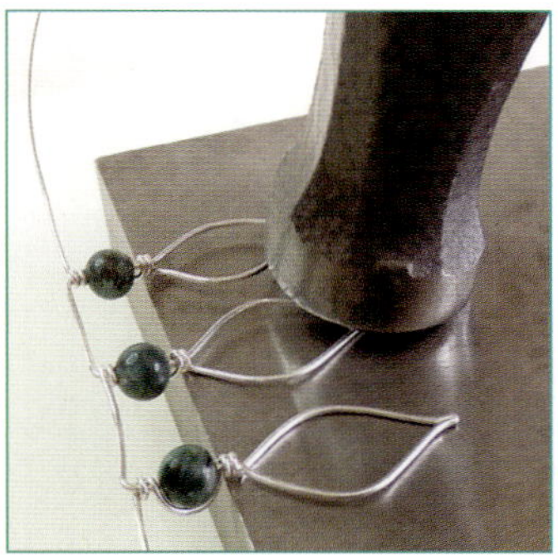

STEP 8

Place the wire piece up to the edge of a stainless steel bench block so that the beads and wrapped wire hang over the edge and the front of the wire piece is facing up. Gently hammer all over the leaves to fix the shape. Then concentrate more hammering on the sides of the leaves to spread the wire.

STEP 9

Make two small loops in the remaining wire either side of the wire piece by wrapping the wire around round nose pliers. Cut off the excess wire and gently hammer each small loop to fix the shape. To remove any tool marks and give the piece a shiny finish, rub the piece over with different grade emery papers (rough to smooth) and then polish the piece with a polishing cloth. Finally, carefully open up the small loops and attach the wire piece to a chain necklace.

Extra Project Make earrings

Make a matching pair of falling leaf earrings from approx. 5" of wire for each earring. Form leaf shapes and wrap the wire twice above each leaf (as in Steps 1 to 3). Feed a bead down the other wire, create a loop at the top and wrap the wire twice above the bead. Cut off the excess wire and hang the leaves on earwires.

MYSTIC AMMONITE

By Jayne Rimington

Mystic agate is a semiprecious stone that has an unusual appearance. The pattern in different shades of brown, along with grey and white appears to be like a shell. Combine these beads with wire coils to create a simple fossilized shell style pendant.

MATERIALS

- 20mm x 40mm mystic agate bead with 2.5mm hole
- 4mm bead (to coordinate with mystic agate)
- 26 gauge (0.4mm) gunmetal-colored copper wire
- 20 gauge (0.8mm) gunmetal-colored copper wire
- 3mm antique copper spacer beads
- Antique copper jumprings
- Antique copper spring cord ends
- Antique copper toggle clasp
- 2mm brown leather cord
- Basic jewelry tools

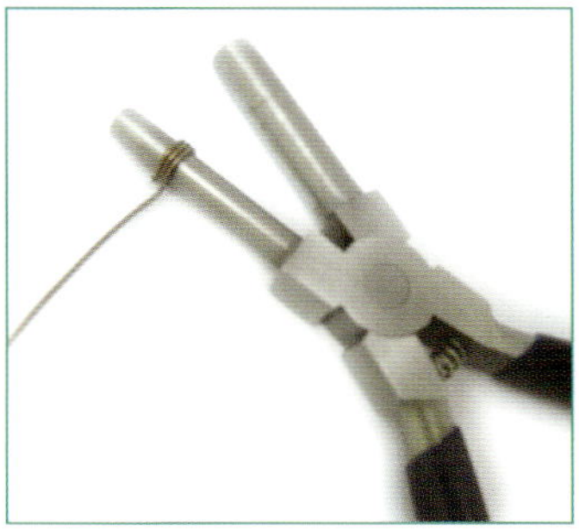

STEP 1
Cut approximately 12" of 20 gauge wire. Starting at the end of the wire and using either round nose pliers or bail maker pliers coil three loops to make the bail of the pendant. Use flat nose pliers to bend the remaining wire at a 90 degree angle downwards.

STEP 2
Next thread on the 4mm bead to sit under the bail and then thread on the mystic agate bead. Pull the wire taut so there are no gaps between the bail and bead. Bend the remaining wire around the oval shape of the bead.

STEP 3
Use round nose pliers to curl up from the end of the wire to make a swirl shape. Adjust the swirl shape to fit the top of the bead, you can do this either with pliers or you may prefer to do this by hand.

PHOTOGRAPHS: LAUREL GUILFOYLE, JAYNE RIMINGTON

STEP 4
Cut approximately 12" of 26 gauge wire. Starting at the base of the 20 gauge wire under the agate bead wind around three to four times, keeping the wire taut. Thread on a copper spacer bead, wrap wire around another three times and repeat until you reach the top of the agate bead.

STEP 5
Secure the last spacer bead by a few wire wraps then finish the end of the wire by wrapping a few times under the small bead under bail. Trim and tuck the end of the wire. Cut the required length of leather cord for the necklace allowing for the clasp. Add the pendant to the leather cord.

STEP 6
Attach spring cord ends onto the leather by carefully squeezing the last lower coil with chain nose pliers. Finish off the necklace with a clasp by using jumprings to attach the clasp to the spring cord ends.

Extra Projects Make earrings and a bracelet

EARRINGS
A pair of matching earrings can be made using the wire swirl shape. Create the swirl then hammer the shape to make it more rigid. Create another swirl in the opposite direction at the other end of the wire for the top of the earrings. Wire wrap spacer beads around the shape as before. Complete by adding jumprings and attach to earwires.

BRACELET
Cut a bracelet length of leather cord and thread a focal agate bead on. Cut approximately 12" of 20 gauge wire. Use round nose pliers to make a swirl like the pendant and attach by wrapping three times around the leather above the bead hole. Shape the wire around the bead and wrap again three times on the other side of the bead. Cut excess wire and neaten with pliers. Cut 26 gauge wire and wrap spacer beads onto wire shape and secure as with the pendant. Add cord ends, jumprings and a clasp.

BEAUTIFUL WIRE NECKLACE

By Sian Hamilton

Frame your favourite lampwork bead with copper wire for an elegant pendant.

MATERIALS

- 18 gauge (1mm) copper wire
- 22 gauge (0.6mm) copper wire
- Focal bead
- 6mm copper jumpring
- Copper chain with clasp
- Steel block
- Hammer with flat head
- Wire cutters
- Small file or emery paper
- Liver of sulphur (optional)
- Ring mandrel (optional)

Designer tips

- After finishing this piece I used Liver of sulphur to darken it a little as I like the way that makes the bead show up more. You can decide whether you like the look of the bright copper or want to darken it a bit.
- If leaving your pendant in its natural copper color you will need to use a product like Renaissance Wax to coat the wire to stop it discoloring in the future.

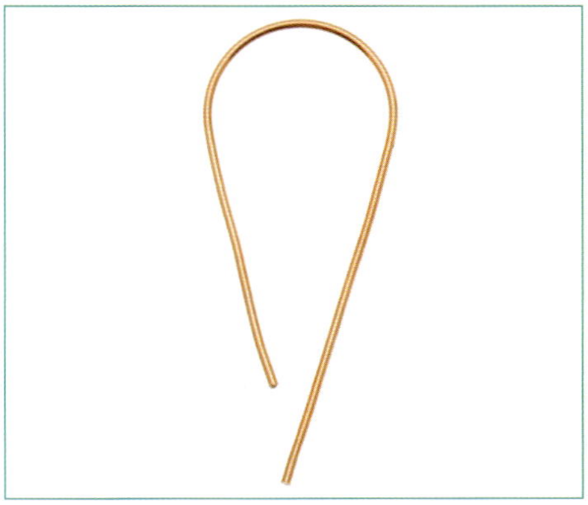

STEP 1

Take a piece of 18 gauge copper wire and cut a 6" length. Bend the wire around a ring mandrel or something else with about a 1" diameter, making one end longer than the other.

STEP 2

Using a small file or emery paper, sand the ends to round them off. On a steel block hammer the ends until they flatten. This is not essential but I think it gives a nice finish.

PHOTOGRAPHS: LAUREL GUILFOYLE, SIAN HAMILTON

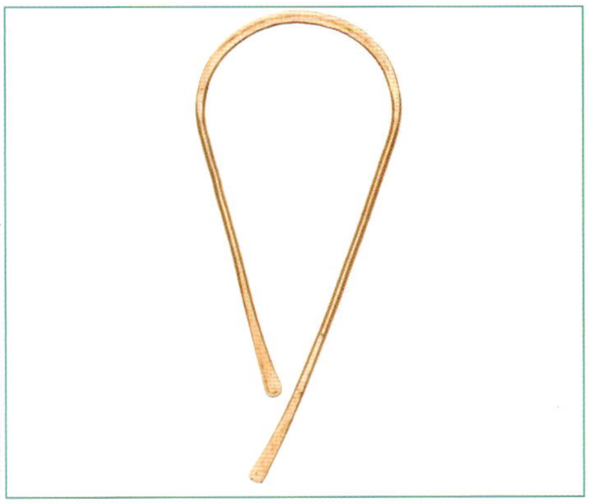

STEP 3

On the steel block, hammer the top curve; stop where the wire starts to go down each side. Hammering like this adds strength but don't go crazy or the wire will weaken.

STEP 4

To add the bead to the center, take a 12" length of 22 gauge wire and coil it around one side of the copper shape. Thread the bead on in the center of the shape.

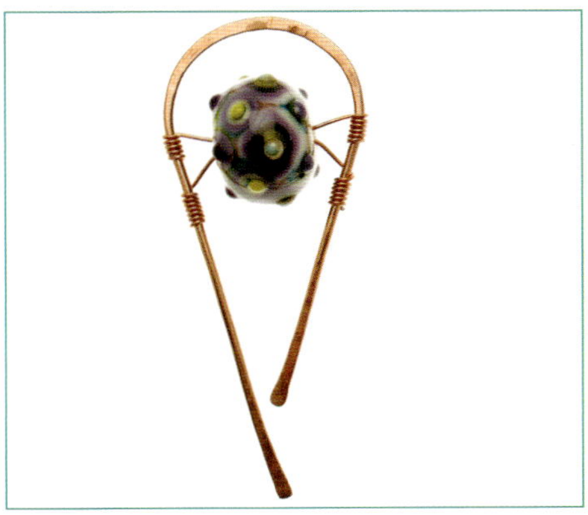

STEP 5

Coil on the opposite side to secure the bead. Cut off the excess wire and make another coil lower down the wire. Feed through the bead and coil on the opposite side. This will secure the bead so it stays in the center of the shape.

STEP 6

Slightly flatten the jumpring and wire it to the top of the curve. Coil twice on the curve then once around the jumpring, once around the curve then once around the jumpring, repeat once more and finish with two wraps around the curve. Add a chain to the jumpring to finish.

Extra Project Make earrings

Use the main steps to make earrings in this same style. I used two matching focal beads. Make sure you make two copper shapes at the same time so your earrings match. To make these a little different I wrapped the 22 gauge wire in different places so that the beads sat at an angle. You can experiment with the wrapping, as it's easy to undo and rewrap. Add an earwire to the top to finish.

WIRE WRAPPED BEADED NECKLACE

By Clair Wolfe

Take a simple technique and create a multitude of visually impacting jewelry from necklaces to bracelets and pendants.

MATERIALS

- 20 gauge (0.8mm) silver-plated wire
- Selection of beads
- Clasp
- Jumprings
- Basic jewelry tools

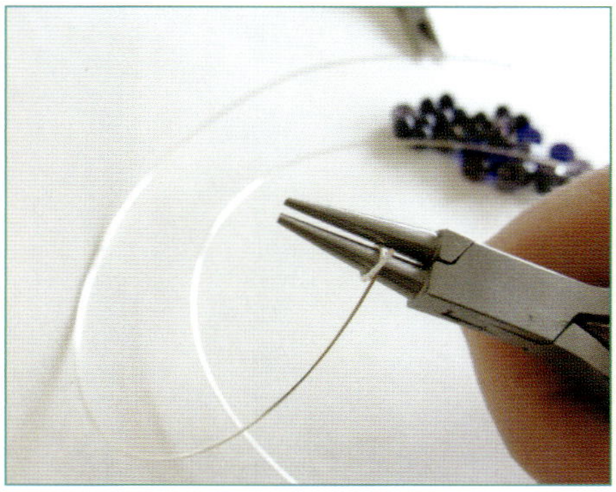

STEP 1

Cut a long length of 20 gauge silver-plated wire around twice the length the finished necklace will be, longer if you can manage. Use a pair of round nose pliers to create a loop in the last 3/4" of one of the ends of wire.

STEP 2

Hold the loop between a pair of flat nose pliers so that it keeps its shape, and then wind the tail around to create a coil. Thread a selection of beads onto the length of wire. Add a second loop at the point along the wire that will become the finished necklace length.

STEP 3

Create another coil, as in Step 2 with the remaining length of wire. Do not trim the excess; this will be used for the first run of wrapping. Pass the first bead up along the wire to the coil and then pass the remaining wire length over this bead and wrap a couple of times.

PHOTOGRAPHS: LAUREL GUILFOYLE, CLAIR WOLFE

STEP 4

Pass the next bead up along the wire, but this time add a selection of beads to the remaining wire length before passing over the beads and wrapping. Continue this with each of the beads added in Step 2. Once you reach the coiled end, wrap a couple of times, snipping away any excess wire. Use needle nose pliers to tuck the cut end away neatly.

STEP 5

Cut another length of 20 gauge wire, once again as long as you can comfortably manage to use. Secure at one of the coiled ends by wrapping around a few times and tucking in the end with pliers. Continue to add beads and wrap, adding beads of different colors, sizes and finishes. Add as many of these runs as you like until you are happy with the look of the wire wrap.

STEP 6

Once the last wire has been wrapped, snipped and tucked into place with pliers, the beaded wrapped length can be shaped. Use your hands to gently curve the length into a circle; this is very easy to do as the structure is quite flexible. Finally add a clasp of your choice.

Project Variations

This style of wirework also looks great as a bracelet or pendant. It can be made with bigger beads or as a delicate piece with finer wire and seedbeads. The possibilities are endless!

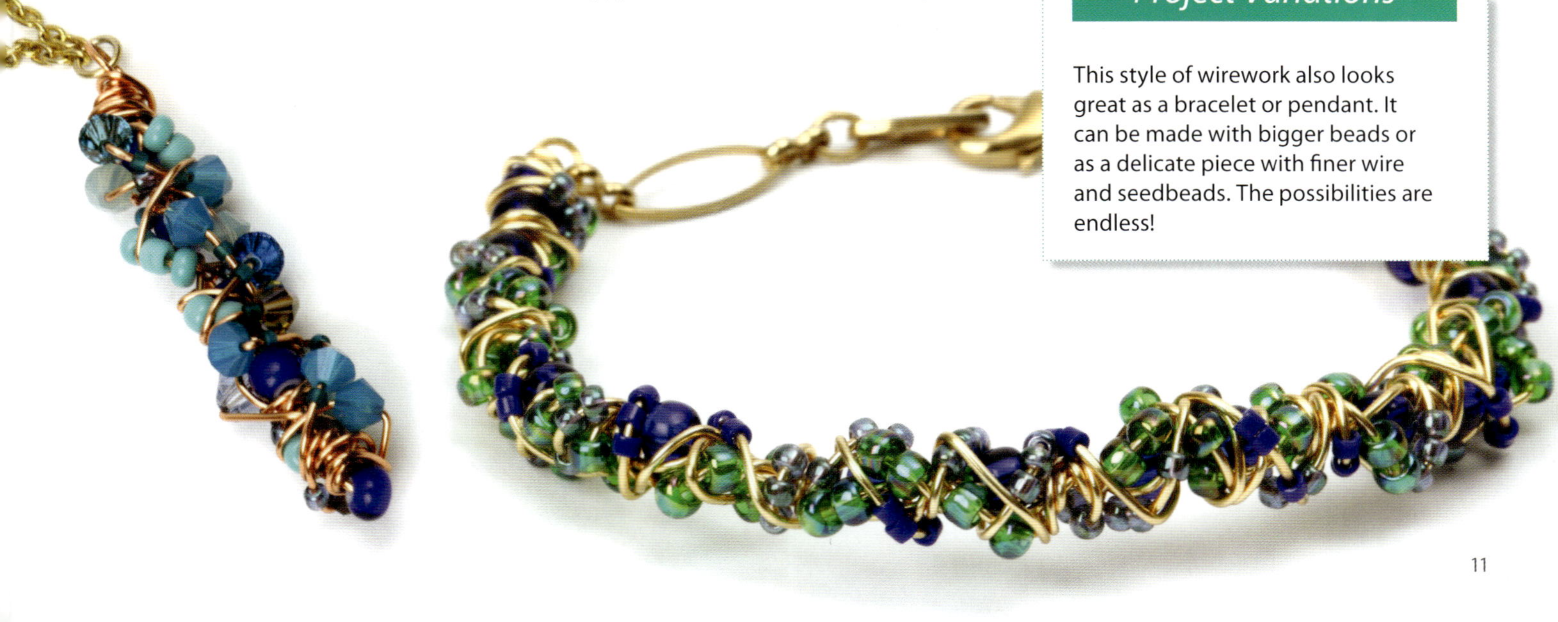

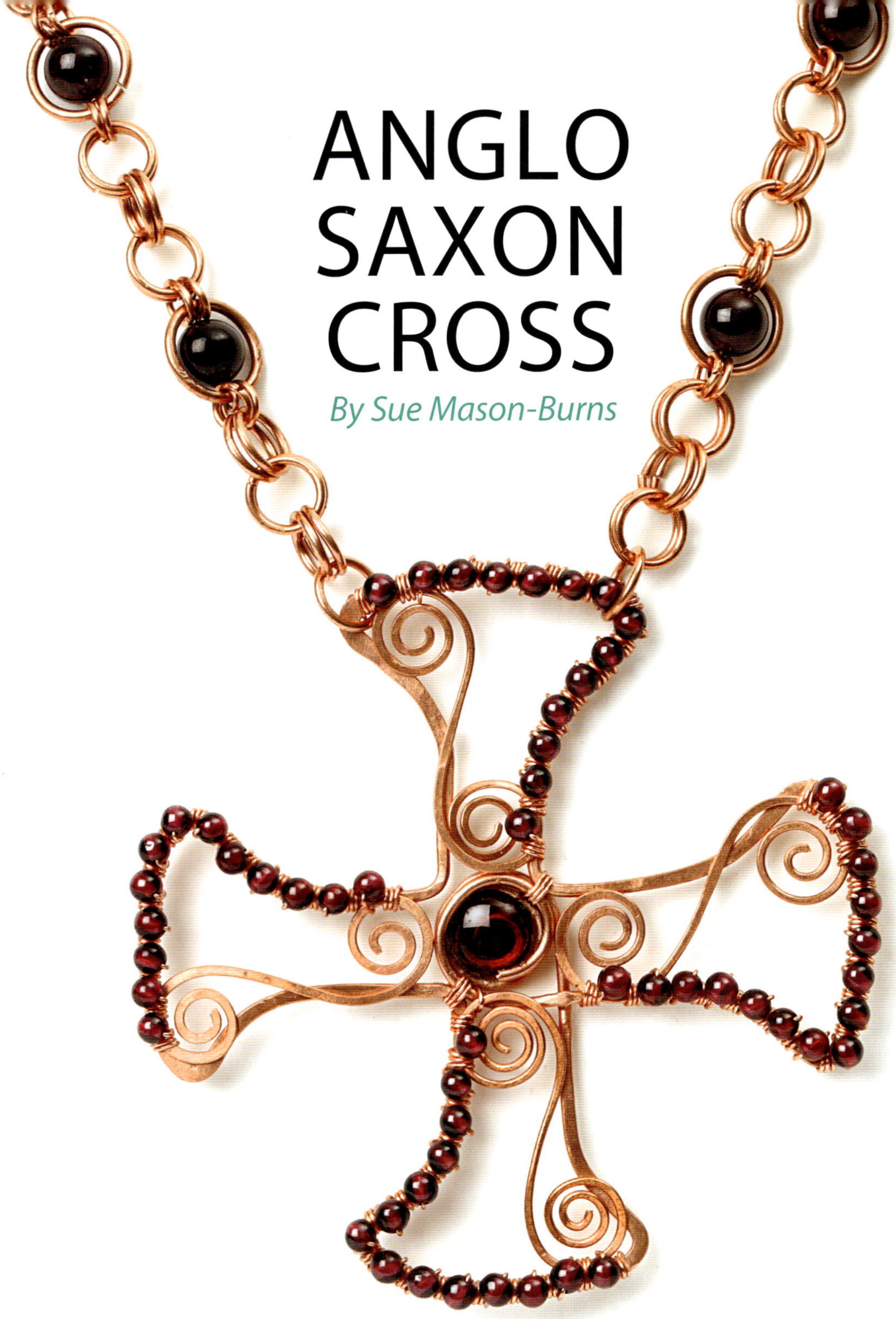

ANGLO SAXON CROSS

By Sue Mason-Burns

This necklace was inspired by the Staffordshire Hoard – the largest hoard of Anglo Saxon gold ever found. Decorate the cross with a center of garnet and filigree spirals for extra detail.

MATERIALS

- 16 gauge (1.25mm) copper wire
- 20 gauge (0.8mm) copper wire
- 26 gauge (0.4mm) copper wire
- 8mm garnet cabochon
- 3mm garnet rounds
- 7mm garnet rounds
- 16 gauge copper jumprings (inside diameter 8.6mm)
- 18 gauge copper jumprings (inside diameter 5.7mm)
- 20 gauge copper jumprings (inside diameter 4mm)
- Copper eye pins
- Copper toggle clasp
- Soft cloth
- Renaissance Micro-Crystalline Wax Polish
- Low tack masking tape
- Zap® gel jewelry glue
- Basic jewelry tools
- Chasing hammer
- Steel bench block

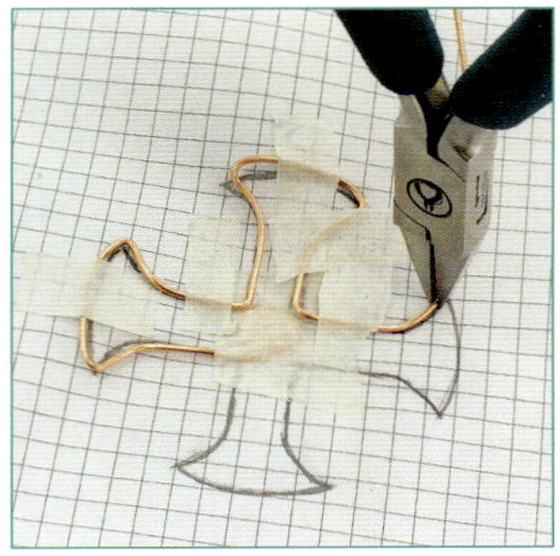

STEP 1

Draw out the shape of your cross as a template. Cut a 24" length of 16 gauge wire and form a closed spiral in one end big enough for the cabochon plus one coil of wire. Tape the spiral to the center of the template. Form the wire into the shape of the template, taping in place as you go to hold the shape in place.

STEP 6

Secure the opposite end of the spiral shape and finish with the three coils of 26 gauge wire at the apex of the bend in the cross. Trim and secure the wire. Repeat Step 5 for the remaining three arms of the cross, being consistent with the bead placement on each arm.

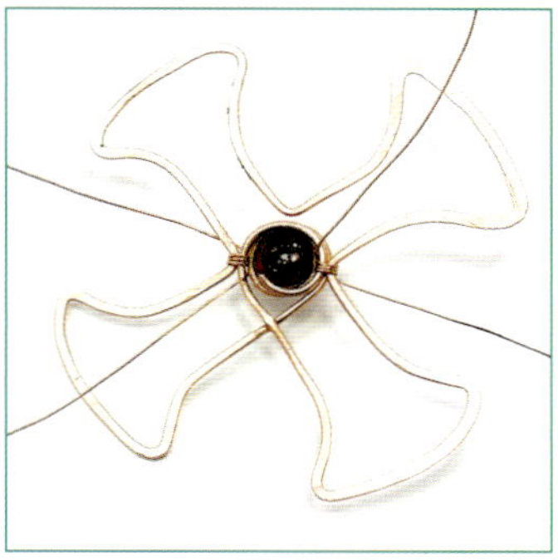

STEP 2
Leave the excess tail wire in place. Use a steel bench block and chasing hammer to forge the cross shape flat. Glue the cabochon in place in the center of the spiral and allow to set. Form the remaining tail wire from Step 1 around the outside of the cabochon, covering the outer layer of the spiral, and trim.

STEP 3
Cut two 78" lengths of 26 gauge wire. Find the center of each wire and wrap these three times around the outer wires of the spiral and the corners of the cross shape. Leave the tails in place.

STEP 4
Cut four 3$\frac{1}{4}$" lengths of 16 gauge wire. Form open, decorative spirals in each end of this piece of wire in opposite directions. Hold the spirals up to your cross design as you form the spirals to make sure that they fit the space. Use the bench block and chasing hammer to forge these shapes flat.

STEP 5
Lay a spiral shape within an arm of the cross. Use a 26 gauge wire tail to secure the spiral in place by coiling around both three times. Thread on a 3mm garnet bead and coil once around the cross frame, coil three times and add another bead. Continue adding beads in this way along one side of an arm of the cross and the end of the arm.

PHOTOGRAPHS: LAUREL GUILFOYLE, SUE MASON-BURNS

STEP 7
Use a soft cloth to apply a coat of Renaissance Wax to all of the exposed copper. Apply sparingly and buff to a soft sheen. The wax will seal the wire and prevent it from tarnishing. If you prefer to add a patina with liver of sulphur for a darker copper look, do this now, then add the Renaissance Wax to seal the patina.

STEP 8
Thread 7mm beads onto eye pins and make simple loops. Link together three sets of two 5.7mm jumprings. Attach two 4mm jumprings to the last two rings in the set of three. Thread an 8.6mm jumpring through one 4mm jumpring, one loop of a bead, the other 4mm ring, and the other loop of the bead, close the ring. Add two 4mm rings to the 8.6mm ring either side of the bead.

STEP 9
Add the first two rings of the next set of three 5.7mm rings to the 4mm rings added at Step 8. Continue in this way until you have two equal lengths of chain. Attach each length to the cross at each corner of one arm with a 5.7mm jumpring and add a toggle clasp to each side of the opposite end of the chain with 5.7mm jumprings.

Extra Projects Make a fibula pin and a bracelet

FIBULA PIN
File one end of a length of 16 gauge wire to a point. Form three coils (which act as a spring) around a mandrel at the end of the length of the pin. Form a catch to tuck the pin behind, then begin forming decorative spirals with the remaining wire. Finish by adding 3mm beads with 26 gauge wire and form into a spiral with a 7mm garnet as the center.

BRACELET
Follow the instructions for the chain maille chain in the necklace project and make a length suitable for a bracelet. Add a matching toggle clasp.

RAINBOW DREAMS

By Annemarie Kenyeres

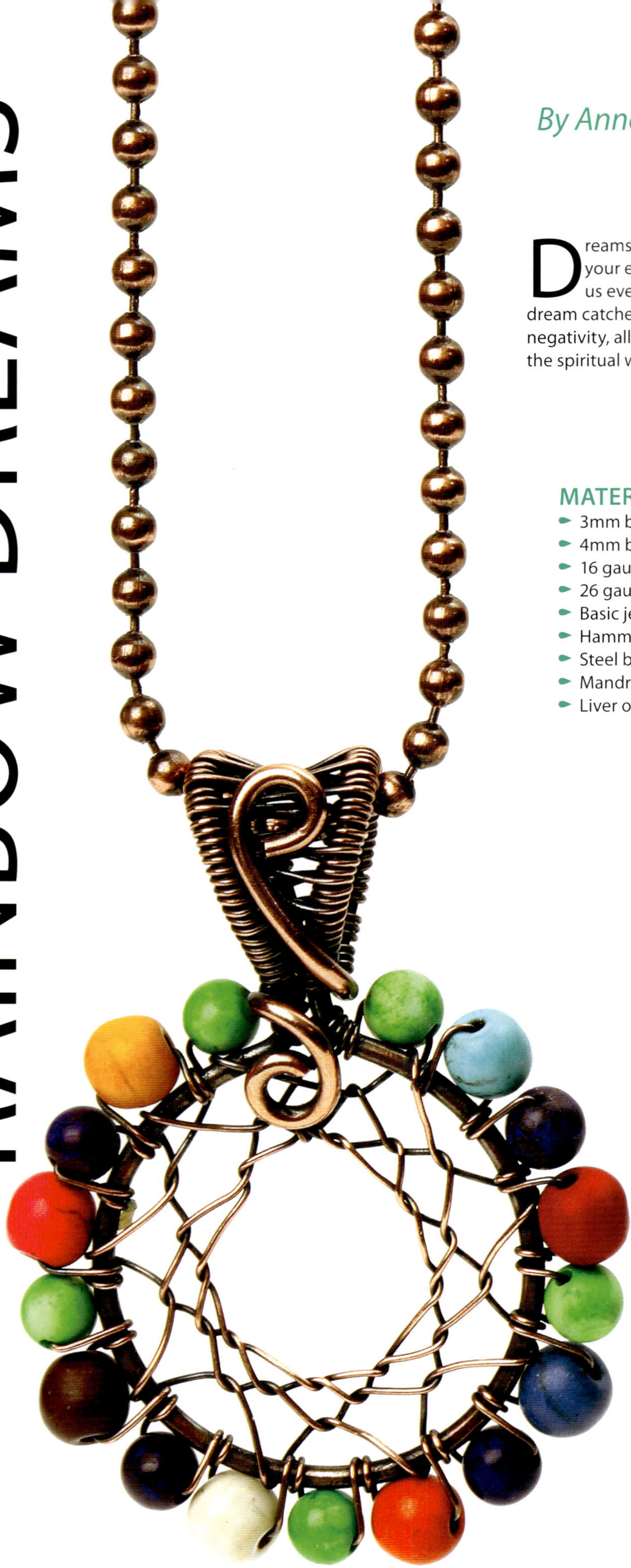

Dreams don't just exist when the sun is down and your eyes are shut; we carry our dreams with us everywhere. In Native American folklore, the dream catcher protects its wearer from nightmares and negativity, allowing only positive dreams to drift from the spiritual world into the mind.

MATERIALS

- 3mm beads
- 4mm beads
- 16 gauge (1.25mm) copper wire
- 26 gauge (0.4mm) copper wire
- Basic jewelry tools
- Hammer
- Steel block
- Mandrel
- Liver of Sulphur (optional)

Designer tips

- Use a larger mandrel and larger beads to create a dream-catcher to hang from your window.
- Dip your finished pieces in Liver of Sulphur to get the antiqued effect. Polish the high sections to highlight the intricate wirework.
- Add extra beads to the dream catcher by threading them onto the wire when creating the loops around the inside of the frame.

STEP 1

Cut a length of 16 gauge wire and shape it around a cylindrical mandrel. Continue to shape the circle until the ends cross over each other in the center. Place the tip of your chain nose pliers on the outside of where the wires cross over and create a right angle in each wire. Straighten both wires so they sit parallel to each other. Work-harden with a hammer and block.

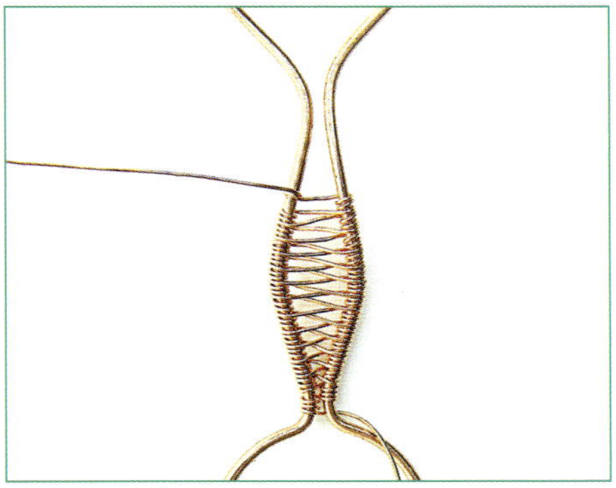

STEP 2

Cut a long length of 26 gauge wire and wrap three times to secure it to one of the bail wires. Cross over to the other side and wrap three times. Continue this wrapping pattern halfway up the bail. Use your thumb to gently curve each bail wire before continuing to wrap to the end of the bail wires. Cut the end of the 26 gauge wire and secure.

STEP 3

Shape the bail by bending the woven section, back over and around something cylindrical, such as a pencil. Separate the wires so the woven section touches the frame. Bend both wires to the front of the piece. Thread a 3mm bead onto the 26 gauge wire, hold it still on the frame and secure it by wrapping once around the frame. Add another bead. Repeat this until beads surround the frame.

PHOTOGRAPHS: LAUREL GUILFOYLE, ANNEMARIE KENYERES

STEP 4

Using the remaining 26 gauge wire, wrap three times around the opposite side of the bail to secure. Create the outer loops by bringing the 26 gauge wire over the opposite side. On every second bead, thread the wire from the front to the back, between the bead and the frame. Bring the wire back through to the front and repeat this until you have loops all around the inside of the frame.

STEP 5

Return to the center and thread the wire through the front of the first loop. Pull tight (not too tight to distort the loop) then bring the wire back through to the front. You can see from the image that the second lot of weaving is basically threading the wire over and under each of the first set of loops. Keep each wire taut and continue to wrap through each loop.

STEP 6

When you reach the beginning, continue to thread the wire through each loop from front to back. Keep taut by placing your finger on the wire before threading it back through to the front of the piece. Continue to do this until you have two more full rotations. Cut the end and secure it to one of the loops. Use pliers to create a swirl with the bail wires.

Extra Projects
Make earrings and a ring

EARRINGS

Using a smaller mandrel, create the circle shape and wrap one of the wires around the other to secure them. Secure the 26 gauge wire and weave the dream catcher as before, adding the bead at the finish. Secure the end. Curl the ends of the frame wire and add earwires.

RING

Using a smaller mandrel, create the frame in the same way as the pendant. Leave a tail and weave the shank in the same way, before weaving the dream catcher section. Thread on a 3mm bead to the center of the web before securing the end. Shape around a ring mandrel.

STATEMENT CHOKER

By Annemarie Kenyeres

Bright and bold yet amazingly delicate, this piece is equally wearable for day, night, on the beach or in a magical, mythical forest.

MATERIALS

- Copper wire:
  20" length 12 gauge (2mm)
  20" length 18 gauge (1mm)
  roll of 26 gauge (0.4mm)
- 1 x 4mm bead
- 1 x 20mm drilled coin bead
- Basic jewelry tools
- Chasing hammer
- Steel block
- Small file or emery paper
- Renaissance Micro-Crystalline Wax Polish
- Soft cloth
- Liver of sulphur
- Necklace mandrel

STEP 1

Take the 20" of 12 gauge copper wire. Find the center and create a small loop. Place the wire onto your bench and shape around the coin bead, crossing over at the top center point. Use a steel block and chasing hammer to flatten the frame and gently tap the bottom loop, taking care not to hit any crossed wires, as this will weaken the wire.

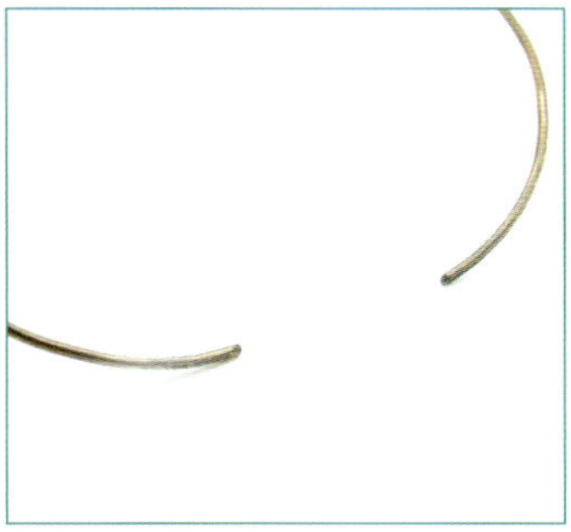

STEP 2

Use a necklace mandrel to shape the choker before using a chasing hammer to first flatten and then work-harden the neck piece. Once you have a basic shape, use the ball end of the hammer to create texture around the neckline. Cut the ends, leaving around a 2" gap in between. Flatten the ends and file to a smooth finish. Wet and dry paper will give you a professional finish.

STEP 3

Thread your coin bead onto the center of the 20" of 18 gauge copper wire. Secure to both sides of the larger loop on the front of the frame by wrapping once tightly on either side. Wrap again, this time taking the wire in a diagonal line up the frame before finishing with the wire on the top of your frame ready to create the woven section.

STEP 4

Shape the 18 gauge wire into a gentle curve that tapers at the end. Secure a length of 26 gauge copper wire onto the 12 gauge wire frame on the left side. Take the 26 gauge wire across and over the back of the 18 gauge wire, wrap three times before crossing and wrapping three times on the 12 gauge wire. Continue this weave until you reach the end of your tapered section. Repeat on the right side.

STEP 5

Gently curve the 18 gauge wire towards the bead and back out, over the top of the 12 gauge wire. Wrap again to secure, before taking the wire in a gentle curve up the back of the woven section and over to the front, finishing just inside the first loop. Now take the 18 gauge wire down over the bead and secure to the base of the frame. Repeat on the other side.

STEP 6

Use the remaining 26 gauge wire on each side to secure the curve, finishing on the 12 gauge frame. Wrap a few times, snip and secure. Repeat this on the other side. Take a length of 26 gauge wire and secure to one side of the bottom loop. Thread on the 4mm bead and secure to the other side. Snip and tuck away the end. Once finished apply patina and polish.

Extra Projects Make a toe ring and bangle

TOE RING

Using 16 gauge wire, create a loop and shape around a ring mandrel or thick marker pen. File the ends. Attach a bead on top of the loop (sitting flat on the frame) with 26 gauge wire wrapping a few times around the frame on either side. Snip and tuck in the ends.

BANGLE

Follow the same steps as the main project but using a bracelet mandrel. Wrap the remaining 18 gauge wire along the length of the bangle. Attach another length of 18 gauge wire to the top of the frame, bring both ends down the bead and secure to the bottom of the frame. Curl up the front of the wires.

EGYPTIAN SPIRALS BRACELET

By Tansy Wilson

Use colored wire to create a fun and vibrant bracelet using a style of linking called the Egyptian spiral.

MATERIALS

- Round nose pliers
- Nylon nose pliers
- 18 gauge (1mm) wire in various colors

Extra Project
Make earrings

Make a pair of earrings in the same way as you made the links of the bracelet, changing the lengths of the wire for each pair of spirals. Start with 6" for the top pair, then 8" for the second pair and finally 10" for the bottom pair. Make a single spiral of wire to hang from the very bottom. Link all together and then form an earring hook to join these to.

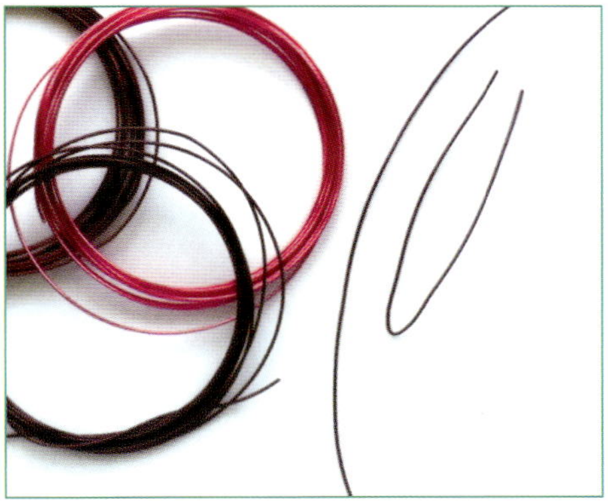

STEP 1

Use 18 gauge wire in any color of your choice or use a selection of colors. For an average sized wrist, cut 21 lengths of wire, each one 6" long. Bend each wire in half.

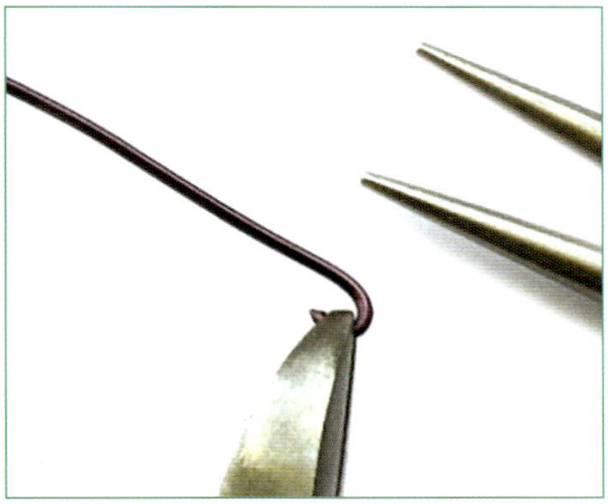

STEP 2

Take one of your folded 6" lengths and hold one end of the wire in the tip of your round nose pliers and start to form a loop. Cut the very end of the wire off then continue to form a perfect circle. Repeat this to the other end of the wire.

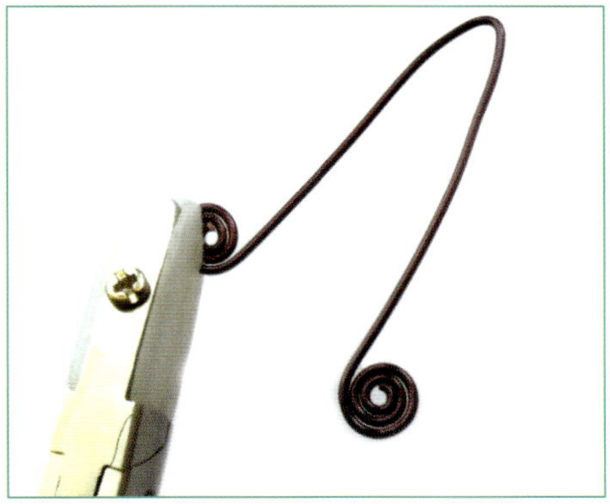

STEP 3

Now hold one of the circles in the jaws of your nylon nose pliers. Start to bend the wire tightly around itself, forming a spiral. Repeat this for the other end of the wire.

PHOTOGRAPHS: LAUREL GUILFOYLE, TANSY WHEELER

STEP 4

Continue to form spirals on each end until you are left with approximately $^{3}/_{4}$" of straight wire from the halfway point (#1, above). Hold both spirals in your nylon jaw pliers and bend the wire just under the spirals at 90 degrees (#2, above). Remove pliers and continue to fold the wire back on itself until it nearly touches the straight part of the wire (#3, above).

STEP 5

Repeat Steps 2–4 so you make 21 spiral links in total. Take one link and thread the straight loop of wire through the straight loop of wire on another link. Keep repeating this step so you link all 21 together.

STEP 6

Finally add a clasp. I made a very simple shepherd's hook clasp so it matches the colored wire. Form a spiral at the end of the hook so that it just fits through a handmade double jumpring to make a secure fastening.

BRAIDED COPPER BRACELET

By Sue Mason-Burns

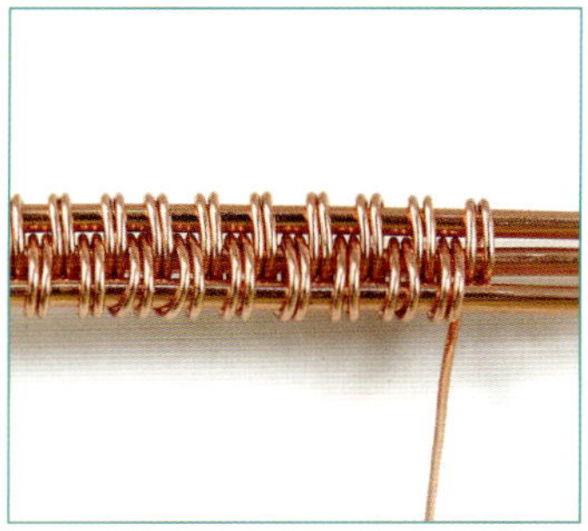

STEP 1

Cut three sets of three 12" lengths of 14 gauge frame wire. Take the first set of three and lay them parallel. Cut a 79" length of 22 gauge wire. Begin 4" from one end and weave as follows: coil twice around the lower two wires together, pass the wire around the center wire and coil twice around the upper two wires together. Pass the wire behind all three wires and repeat.

Use chunky wire to create this eye-catching braided bracelet in glorious copper.

MATERIALS

- 118" of 14 gauge (1.6mm) bare copper wire
- 237" of 22 gauge (0.6mm) bare copper wire
- GS Hypo Cement
- Oval bangle mandrel
- Emery boards in various grades coarse to fine
- Liver of Sulphur
- Renaissance Micro-Crystalline Wax Polish
- Polishing cloth
- Large bail making pliers
- Heavy-duty flush cutters
- Bench vise
- Plastic tweezers
- Basic jewelry tools

Extra Projects
Make a necklace and earrings

NECKLACE

Follow the instructions in the main project to make a 4"-6" length of braid. Gently curve this braid. Make a chain with 5mm and 8mm jumprings, interlinking sets of two rings for each link of the chain. Make sections of five sets of two 5mm jumprings, followed by two 8mm jumprings. Attach to the center loops at each end of the braid and finish with a handmade clasp.

EARRINGS

Make a section of the chain you made for the necklace, with five sets of two 5mm jumprings and finish with an 8mm jumpring. Hang from earwires with a 4mm jumpring.

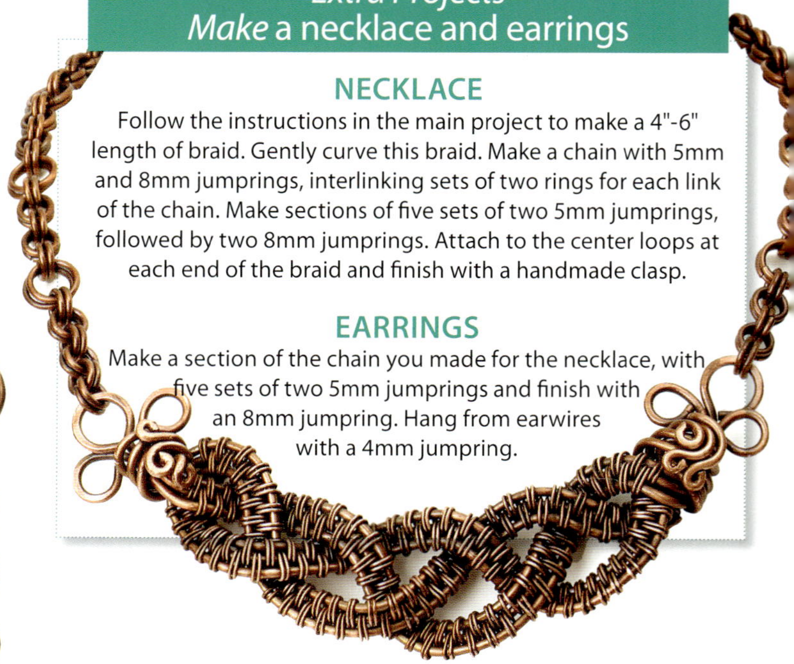

STEP 2

Complete an 8" length of weaving and repeat for the two remaining sets of three wires. Secure all three sections side by side in a vise. Carefully and evenly braid these sections, bringing the outside sections to the center in turn, until all sections are braided. Remove from the vise and fan out the three sets of three unwoven wires, one straight and two at right angles on each side.

STEP 3

Trim and secure all weaving wires. Flatten the tails with flat nose pliers and press against the rear of the frame wires. Add a dab of hypo cement for security. Finish each end of the braid by wrapping each of the two unwoven sets of frame wire (left at right angles in Step 2) around the central set of wires. Wrap each set in turn and leave at right angles to the central wires.

STEP 4

Use round nose pliers to form decorative spirals with the six frame wires, three on each side. Arrange five of the six decorative spirals at the front of the design. Vary the size of the spirals so each end narrows to a slight point. Position the sixth spiral inside the design to cover any messy wirework visible there. Form three simple loops in the remaining unwoven central frame wires.

STEP 5

Form the bracelet shape around an oval bangle mandrel. Start with a larger size, and gradually bring down to the desired final size of the bangle. Press the design firmly against the mandrel with your fingers. Finish by taking the bracelet to a smaller size than required on the mandrel and squeeze the bracelet so the ends cross. The bracelet will spring back to the correct size.

PHOTOGRAPHS: LAUREL GUILFOYLE, SUE MASON-BURNS

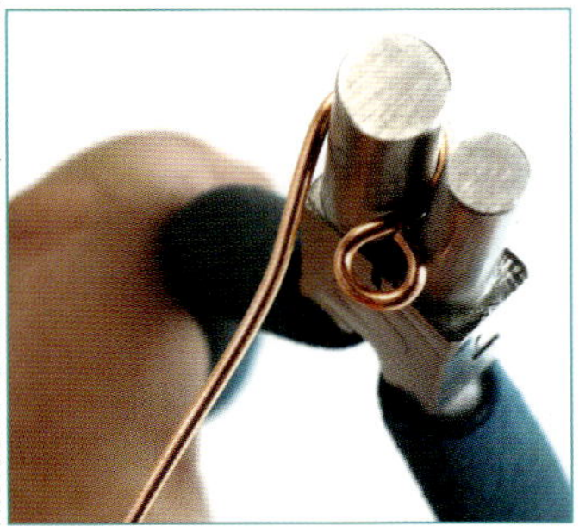

STEP 6

To make the hook clasp, cut a 3$^{1}/_{4}$" length of 14 gauge wire. Form a loop in one end with round nose pliers. Form the hook shape around the larger jaw of large bail making pliers. Trim the end of the hook with flush cutters and use flat nose pliers to bend the last $^{1}/_{4}$" of the hook at a slight angle.

STEP 7

Use a succession of emery boards, ranging from coarse to fine, to sand the tip of the hook until it is smooth. Attach the hook to the center loop at one end of the bracelet. Use the emery boards to sand out any tool marks in the spirals formed at Step 4.

STEP 8

Prepare a solution of Liver of Sulphur and warm water in a non-metallic bowl. Prepare a bowl of cold water in a second non-metallic bowl. Use plastic tweezers to hold the bracelet and dip in the Liver of Sulphur and cold water alternately until you achieve the depth of color you desire. Dipping allows color to build up gradually so that you don't over-oxidize the piece.

STEP 9

Use a polishing cloth to remove some of the oxidation and give a depth of color, which emphasizes the texture of the weaving. Pay close attention to the weaving wire, polishing until it is lighter in color than the frame wires underneath. Polish until you are happy with the color, then use a soft cloth to apply Renaissance Wax to preserve the oxidation and prevent transfer to the skin.

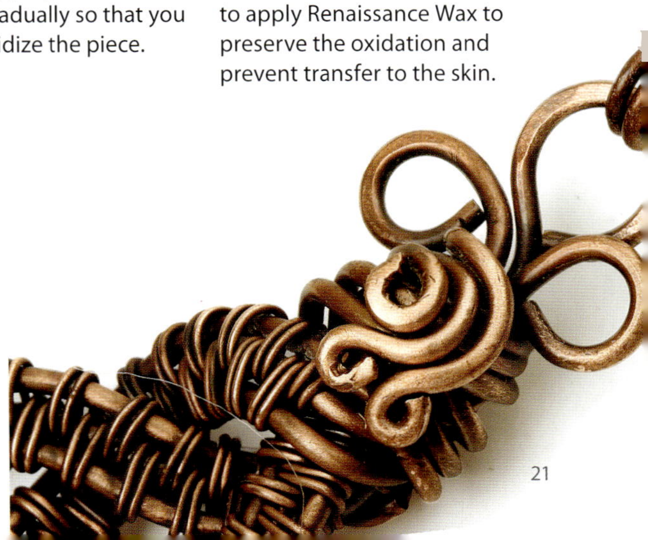

TANGLED WEAVE

By Nicola Beer

Weave a spellbinding wirework necklace in fresh spring hues.

MATERIALS

- 20 gauge (0.8mm) wire
- 26 gauge (0.4mm) wire
- Oval cabochon
- Basic jewelry tools
- Sanding pads or papers
- Liver of Sulphur gel
- Rotary tool and sanding/polishing attachments
- Tumble polishing machine
- Silver polishing cloth

Designer tips

- Experiment with differently shaped cabochons for a completely unique look.
- When creating intricate wirework, use uncoated, bare copper or Sterling silver that can be oxidized and polished to create depth and enhance the work.
- You can adjust the length of the wires to accommodate larger or smaller cabochons.

STEP 5

Trim off any leftover weaving wire. Separate five wires and pull them over to the left. Do the same with the other five wires on the right-hand side. The five wires on each side are going to form the frame of the cabochon. If your bail has flattened slightly, now is a good time to push bail-making pliers through and mold it back into a rounded shape.

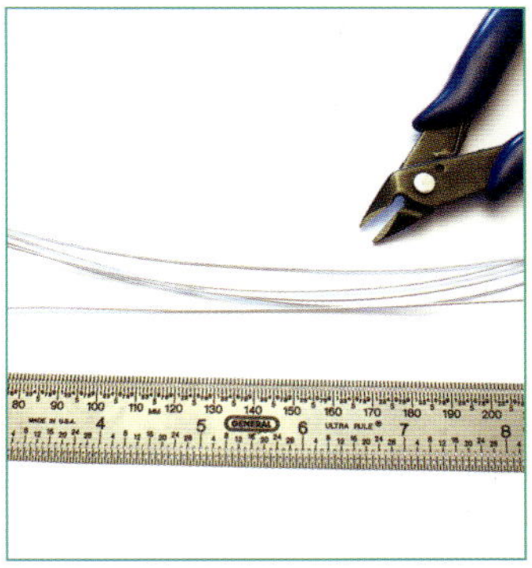

STEP 1

Cut and straighten five 12" lengths of 20 gauge wire. Run the wire lengths gently through your fingers until they are relatively kink-free. They do not need to be perfectly straight and, as this technique works better with nice soft wire, it is important not to work-harden the wire at this stage. It can also be useful to clamp or tape the wires together initially to help with stability.

STEP 2

This wrap starts with the bail by weaving at the center of the five-wire bundle. Take a 79" length of 26 gauge wire and wrap it around the bottom base wire three times to anchor. Continue the weave by passing over and under alternate wires in a basket weave pattern. Weave up the wires until you have completed half of the bail, approx. 1".

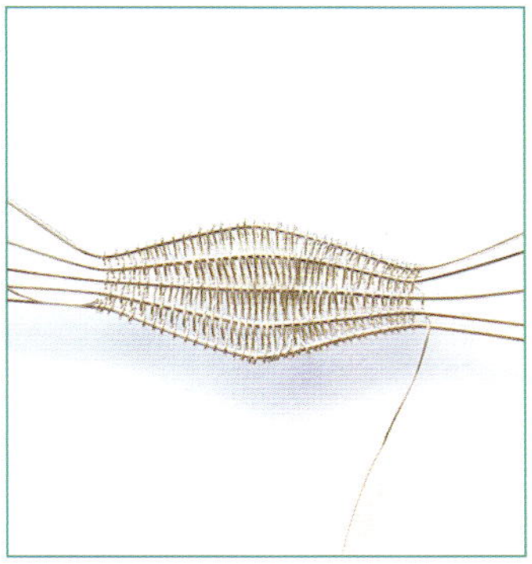

STEP 3

Bend the base wires in slightly to create a diamond shape. Continue weaving down the diamond until it looks symmetrical. Push the weave together to end up with a dense, neat-looking section. You will find that the second half of the bail is more difficult to weave as the wire tends to slip down; take your time and apply even tension to the wire to get it as neat as possible. This comes with practice.

STEP 4

Bend the completed woven section over bail-making pliers to form a loop. On either side of the bail, grasp the wires in a pair of flat nose pliers and bend them outwards at a 90-degree angle, then nip the bail closed. Use the attached weaving wire to tie the bail together and form a closed loop. Use the tail of the weaving wire to coil down one wire for about 2 1/2". Attach a 20" length of 26 gauge wire to an opposite bare wire and coil this wire too.

PHOTOGRAPHS: LAUREL GUILFOYLE, NICOLA BEER

STEP 6

Using just your fingers, interlock and create curls in the five wires at both sides of the bail. The sections at either side should be kept flat so that when they wrap around the cabochon the bail sits upright. Do this in a completely random fashion, keeping both sides the same length and periodically measuring the length of the curls against the length of the cabochon.

STEP 7

Stop just short of the length you think you will need to complete in order for the curled sections to meet at the bottom of the cabochon. Interlock the ends of the wires at the bottom of the cabochon, trim off any excess wire and spiral the ends to secure. Push the spirals into the frame so they disappear into the other curls. Place the cabochon into the frame.

STEP 8

Mold the frame around the edges of the cabochon to form a tangled bezel, by shaping it with your fingers to the front and back of the stone. The wire should be soft enough to shape and the curls can be manipulated until you are happy with the way that they look. It is always better that your frame is a little too tight as there will be lots of 'stretch' in the wire.

STEP 9

Create a chain with basic figure eight loops and accenting gemstone wire wrapped beads. Oxidizing the metal will highlight the intricate wire wrapping, adding depth to the finished piece of jewelry. Make up a solution of Liver of Sulphur with warm water and dip the silver until it turns black. Rinse off the solution and polish the necklace to a high shine in a tumbling machine, with a rotary tool and attachments or with polishing cloths and pads.

GARDEN DELIGHTS

By Sue Mason-Burns

Combine wirework with some very basic Ganutell techniques to create a textured flower choker. Ganutell is the Maltese art of making flowers from wire, floss and beads.

MATERIALS

- 20 gauge (0.8mm) and 26 gauge (0.4mm) non-tarnish silver-plated wire
- Strong 5mm non-tarnish silver-plated jumpring
- Embroidery floss in assorted colors
- Two-hole slider beads
- 24mm flower-shaped trigger clasp
- Basic jewelry tools
- Coiling gizmo
- Large eye needle
- GS Hypo Cement
- Low tack tape
- Electric drill
- Vise
- Necklace mandrel
- Nylon hammer

STEP 1
Use a coiling gizmo to make a length of coiled 20 gauge wire as long as you can make it. Remove the coil from the mandrel and stretch it slightly so that you have a small space between each coil. Cut 3¹/₄" lengths from the coil. Thread the first length onto a 40" length of 20 gauge wire and form a petal. Twist to hold in place and add the next petal.

STEP 2
Repeat until you have a flower shape. Take a 78" length of embroidery floss. Secure one end to the center of the flower. Wind between the wire spirals of a petal. Push the embroidery floss through the large eye needle. Use the needle to pass the floss around the frame at the tip of the petal. Thread around two spirals until you reach the center of the tip of the petal.

STEP 3
Use the needle to weave the embroidery floss along the back of the petal through the coils you made, winding the floss around the spiral frame. At the center of the flower, knot the longer length of floss together securely with the tail of the floss. Repeat with the remaining petals, knotting with the tail of the floss after each petal. Trim and secure each knot with glue.

PHOTOGRAPHS: LAUREL GUILFOYLE, SUE MASON-BURNS

STEP 4
Make a small spiral with the shorter 20 gauge tail wire and press into the rear center of the flower. To add leaves, pull a length of coiled wire slightly further apart to allow more embroidery floss to pass between the coils. Add to the 20 gauge wire and form a leaf shape using chain nose pliers to make the tip. Secure at the center of the flower. Make two leaves in this way.

STEP 5
Attach a length of green floss to the center of the flower and wind up the leaf shape on a diagonal. At the tip of the leaf use the needle to secure around the frame, as you did for the flower petals, and take the floss back down the leaf, creating a crisscross pattern. Secure and repeat for the second leaf. Leave the 20 gauge wire tail for later use.

STEP 6
Thread two lengths of 26 gauge wire through each of the holes in a two-hole slider bead. Position the bead in the center of the flower, with the 26 gauge wire either side of two opposite petals. Turn the flower over and twist all four wires together until the slider bead is secure in position in the center of the flower. Leave the tail wires for later use.

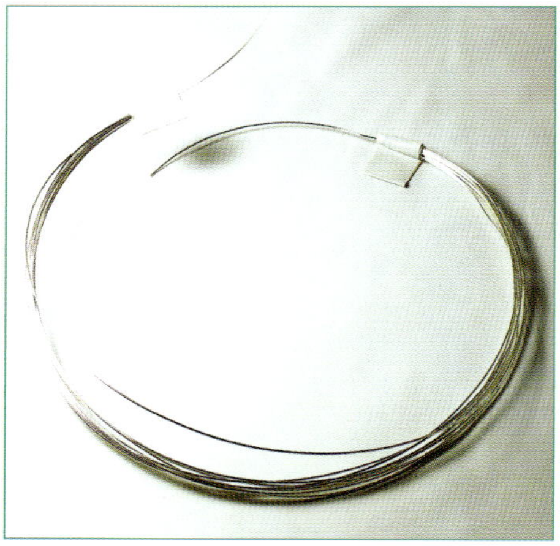

STEP 7

Cut nine 20" lengths and one 28" length of 20 gauge wire. With the longer length in the middle of the bunch, centered with a 4" tail at either end, secure the ends of the shorter wires with tape. Hold one taped end in a vise and the other in the chuck of a drill. Using a slow speed, twist all wires together, leaving the 4" tails straight at either end.

STEP 8

Form a wrapped loop with the 4" tail pieces of wire around the larger end of round nose pliers. Wrap the tail wires around the twisted section for approximately 1/2", trim and secure. Attach the clasp to one of the loops with the jumpring. Use a necklace mandrel and a nylon hammer to form the rounded shape of the neck wire.

STEP 9

Attach the flowers to the neck wire using the 26 gauge and 20 gauge tail wires you left in place when making the flowers. When you are happy the flowers are secure, trim and secure the 26 gauge tail wires. Bring the remaining tails of 20 gauge wire towards the front of the flowers and form open spirals as an additional decoration around the flowers.

Extra Projects Make a brooch and a headband

BROOCH

Make one flower with two leaves, and attach to a small brooch back using the 26 gauge tail wires you used to attach the slider to the center of the flower.

HEADBAND

Make one flower with two leaves, and use the wire tails to attach securely to a tiara headband. Use the remaining 20 gauge tail to make a decorative spiral beside the flower.

RAINBOW BRACELET

By Sue Mason-Burns

Who says less is more? Go over the top with color with this stand-out-from-the-crowd bracelet.

MATERIALS

- 6 x 20mm red green zebra jasper coin beads
- 18 gauge (1.0mm) gunmetal-colored wire
- 28 gauge (0.32mm) gunmetal-colored wire
- 26 gauge (0.4mm) Parawire in various tropical colors
- Basic jewelry tools
- Round bangle mandrel
- Superglue

STEP 1

Cut three 20" lengths of 18 gauge frame wire. Begin a basket weave using 28 gauge wire: coil three times around the lower two wires, pass around the central wire and coil three times around the upper two wires. Complete five sets of three coils. Add a coin bead to the center wire and coil the weaving wire around one of the outer frame wires, splay the outer frame wires out behind the bead.

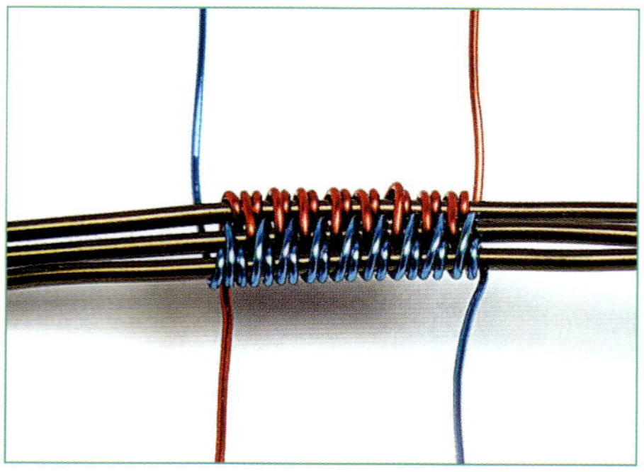

STEP 2

Bring the frame wires back together and repeat the basket weave. Add another coin bead. Repeat for the length of the bracelet. Cut three 31$^{1}/_{2}$" lengths of 18 gauge wire. Working with two different colors of Parawire, begin a weave 4" from the end of the frame: with color 1, coil towards the center, once around an outer wire, once around the outer and center wire and once around the outer wire.

STEP 3

Pick up color 2 and repeat this process, weaving towards the center again, for the remaining outer wire. Repeat this weave, alternating the colors. When your weave is approximately 1" long, wind the tails of the frame wire around the basket weave section before the first bead on your bracelet frame. Curve the weave around the lower half of the bead and continue weaving.

PHOTOGRAPHS: LAUREL GUILFOYLE, SUE MASON-BURNS

STEP 4

When the weave is long enough to reach around half of the coin bead, wind the frame wires around the next basket weave section of the bracelet frame, finishing with the three wires ready to be woven and follow the curve of the upper part of the next bead. Trim and secure the tails of the colored weaving wires. Add a dab of glue to the trimmed and secured tails.

STEP 5

Add two different colored wires, leaving a short tail, and continue weaving as set out in Steps 2 and 3. Follow the upper curve of the coin bead and finish by winding the frame wires around the basket weave section. Repeat this process until all the beads are surrounded with a bi-colored woven frame, alternating the upper and lower curves of the coin beads.

STEP 6

After the last bead, coil the frame wires twice around the last basket weave section of the bracelet frame. Use 28 gauge wire to make the hook section of the clasp. Weave as follows: coil once around the lower frame wire, pass the wire in front of the center and upper wires and coil once around the upper wire, pass behind the three wires. Repeat this weave for 1$^{3}/_{4}$".

STEP 7

Trim each frame wire and form a small loop. Form the woven section into a hook around a mandrel, splaying the three loops at the end of each wire decoratively and to act as the tip of the hook shape. Trim the remaining frame wires and secure firmly to the underside of the bracelet. Add a dab of glue to hold the trimmed tail in place.

STEP 8

Repeat the weave on the wires at the opposite end of the bracelet. Form this woven section into the eye of the clasp around a mandrel. Wind the ends around the frame of the bracelet. Trim each of the remaining frame wires and form into decorative spirals. Press these spirals firmly into the front side of the bracelet with flat nose pliers.

STEP 9

Form the bracelet shape around a round bangle mandrel, or any appropriately sized solid cylindrical shape. Close the clasp and firmly press the beads and their surrounding wire frames into shape. Run your fingers around the inside of the bracelet, checking for loose tail wires. Use a dab of glue to secure any loose ends of colored wire.

Extra Projects Make a necklace and earrings

NECKLACE

Make a centerpiece for a necklace, using the same techniques as the bracelet, with one 20mm coin bead and two 14mm coins either side. Form decorative spirals at either end of the centerpiece, attach two equal lengths of chain and finish with a clasp.

EARRINGS

Add a small rondelle and a 14mm round bead to a headpin and make a loop. Add a tube bead to an eyepin and make a loop. Link together and attach to earwires.

BASIC TECHNIQUES

HOW TO MAKE A WRAPPED LOOP

1. Thread a bead onto a headpin or eyepin. Grip the wire with round nose pliers next to the bead.

2. Bend the wire above the plier jaw to a right angle. You will need about 1/8" of wire above the bead before the bend.

3. Move the plier jaws to sit at the top of the bend.

4. With your thumb push the wire back around the pliers, keeping it tight to the jaw.

5. Keep pushing the wire around the jaw until you meet the bead.

6. Move the pliers around the loop and continue to bend the wire around until it is facing out at a right angle and you have a complete loop.

7. If attaching the loop to a chain this is the stage to do that. Use a pair of chain nose pliers to hold across the loop firmly.

8. Wrap the wire around the neck of the loop until it meets the bead. Snip off any excess wire and push the end against the coil to finish.

PHOTOGRAPHS: SIAN HAMILTON

MAKING A SIMPLE LOOP

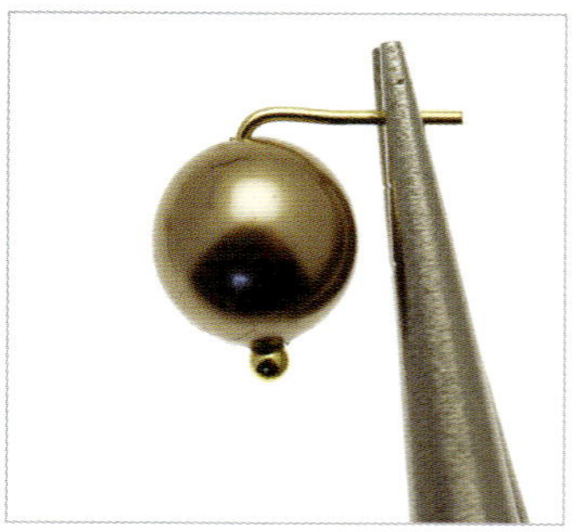

1. Thread the bead onto a headpin or eyepin and cut the pin about 3/8" above the bead. Bend the wire to a right angle above the bead.

2. Using round nose pliers, grasp the wire at the very end and curl it around the plier jaws.

3. Roll the wire around to meet the bead. Bend the loop back to sit directly above the bead.

4. Use chain nose pliers to tighten the loop by twisting it from side to side. Do not pull it outwards as that will distort the shape.

USING JUMPRINGS

Always make sure you follow this guide and don't pull jumprings apart as they can easily distort.

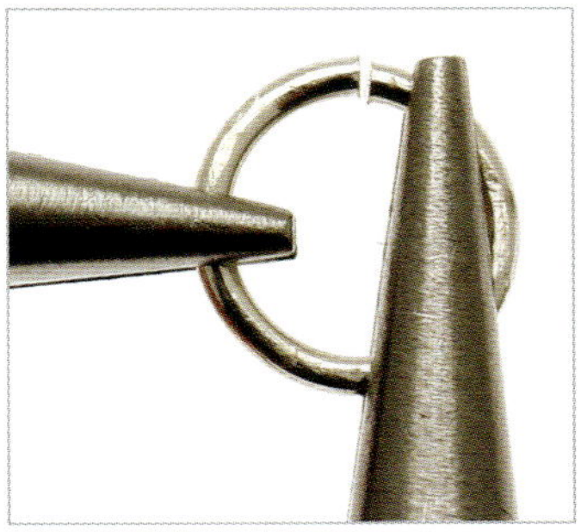

Take a jumpring in two pairs of pliers with the opening centered at the top.

Hold the jumpring either as shown in the step above or this step.

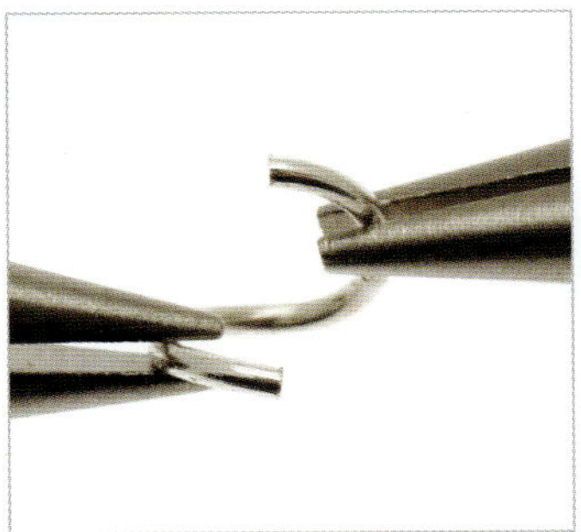

Whichever way you hold the jumpring, the opening motion is the same. Twist one hand towards you and the other hand away; never pull apart. Reverse the action to close.

CRIMPING A BEAD

To show this process clearly it is being shown without using thread; the thread or wire should be inside the crimp bead.

Hold the crimp bead in the pliers with the bead in the hole that has a round side opposite a 'W' shape.

Before closing the pliers, check that the bead is straight. When you close the pliers the thread or wire should fall either side of the bend.

Move the 'U' shape crimp to the other hole with two round sides. Turn the crimp so the 'U' faces sideways and press the pliers closed tightly.

ADDING A COVER

Crimp covers make your finished jewelry look more professional and clean.

Take a crimp cover and place it over the crimped bead, making sure the bead is completely inside the cover.

Take a pair of chain or flat nose pliers and carefully grasp the cover. Gently press the cover closed.

The finished cover should be closed into a perfect bead shape. Nylon nose pliers do this job very well as they won't mark the cover.

MAKING AN EYEPIN

Make your own eyepins using 20 gauge wire. You can use 18 gauge if you need strong pins.

Take the very end of the wire in round nose pliers. If the wire is quite hard it may slip out of the pliers, so start the loop about $^1/_8$" in and snip off the straight piece as you make the first curve.

The shape you want to create is a P. The advantage to making your own eyepins is that you can make the loop any size you need.

To finish the pin so the loop sits centered on the wire, take the round nose pliers and place them where the round P shape meets the wire. Press the wire back against the pliers until the loop is centered.

BASIC TOOLS

TYPES OF PLIERS

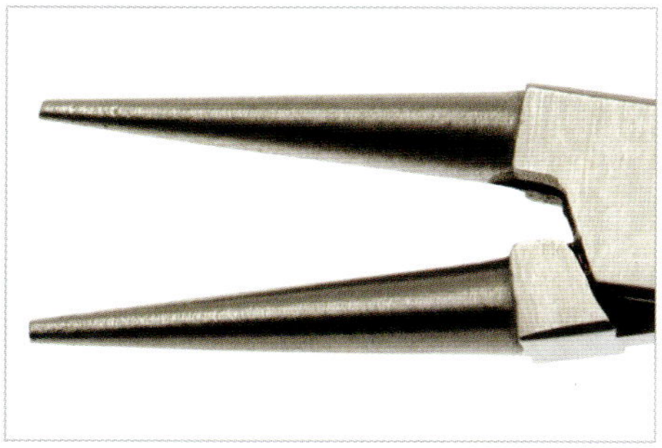

ROUND NOSE

These are a must-have for a basic kit. When making jewelry, being able to create loops and rings is essential.

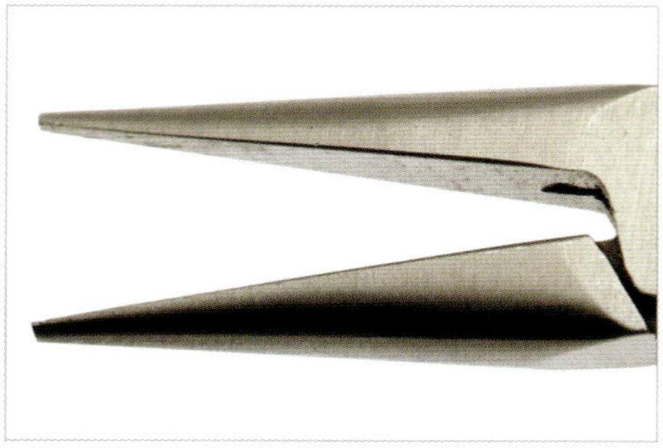

CHAIN NOSE

Also called half round, these are the most versatile. They are used for many jewelry applications, so are another must-have for the basic kit.

FLAT NOSE

Similar to chain nose, these pliers have a wider jaw that is completely flat. Good for holding jumprings/findings as the wide jaw grasps a large area.

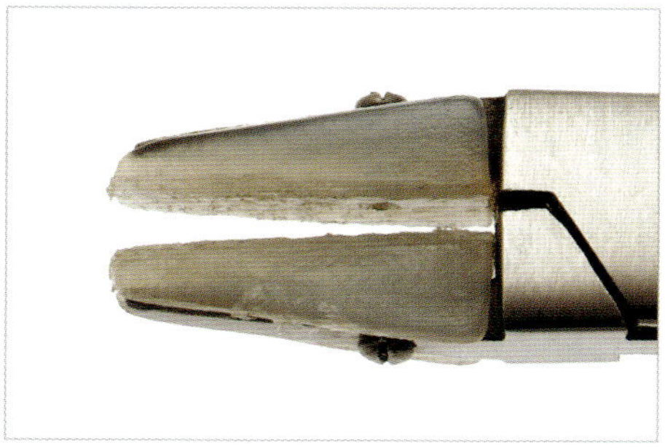

NYLON NOSE

Another similar style to flat nose, these pliers have jaws that are covered in nylon to stop them marking the metal.

BENT NOSE

Used for getting into small tricky spaces where a straight nose pair cannot reach.

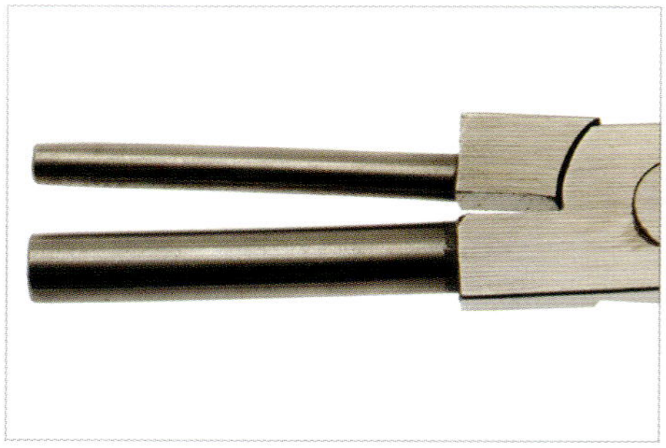

BAIL MAKING

These pliers have fixed sized jaws, with each jaw being a different size, usually with a 2mm difference (such as 3mm and 5mm). They come in a wide variety of sizes and are great if making a lot of the same size jumprings or coils.

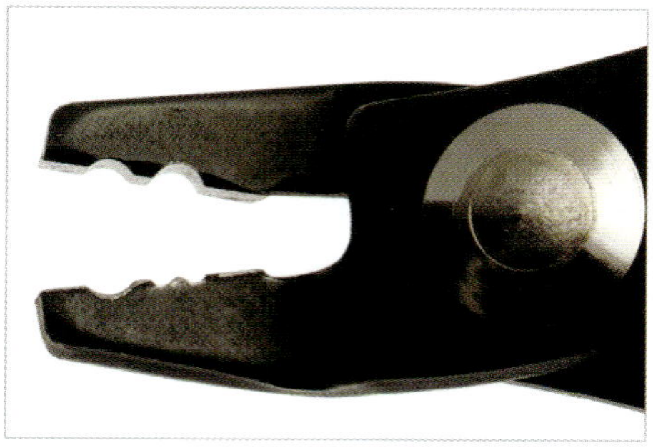

CRIMPING

These pliers are used with crimp beads. If you want to have a nice finish to your crimping then these pliers are a good investment.

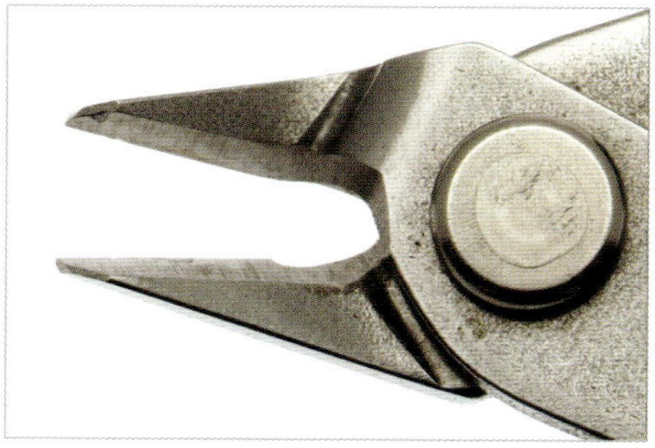

WIRE CUTTERS/SNIPS

These pliers are also called side cutters. They come in a vast range of prices and styles. Be careful what you cut as they can blunt easily if used with hard or large dimension wire.

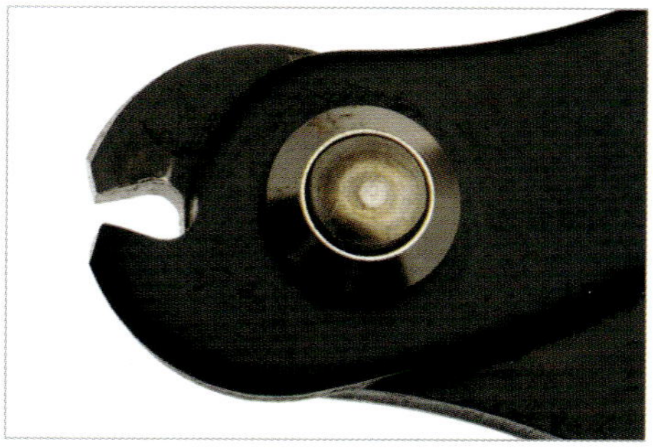

MEMORY CUTTERS

Used exclusively for cutting memory wire. If you are going to use memory wire you must invest in these; the wire will damage standard cutters.